THE SPIDERWICK CHRONICLES

OFFICIAL MOVIE COMPANION

by Wendy Wax
based on the screenplay by
Karey Kirkpatrick and David Berenbaum and John Sayles
from the books by
Tony DiTerlizzi and Holly Black

SIMON AND SCHUSTER

London   New York   Sydney   Toronto

SIMON AND SCHUSTER
First published in Great Britain in 2008 by Simon & Schuster UK Ltd,
Africa House, 64-78 Kingsway, London WC2B 6AH
A CBS company

Originally published in the USA in 2008 by Simon Spotlight,
an imprint of Simon & Schuster Children's Division, New York.

Official movie companion by Wendy Wax; based on books by Tony DiTerlizzi and Holly Black;
screenplay by Karey Kilpatrick and David Berenbaum and John Sayles.

A CIP catalogue record for this book is available from the British Library

ISBN: 978-1-84738-177-4
1 3 5 7 9 10 8 6 4 2
Printed in the United States of America

Table of Contents

Angela DiTerlizzi

FOREWORD

Once upon a time, two talented, imaginative people—author/illustrator Tony DiTerlizzi and writer Holly Black—received a letter from three children who claimed they had seen faeries. Whether this was true or not didn't matter—Tony and Holly, who once shared a passion for the game Dungeons and Dragons, were intrigued.

The letter-writers were Jared Grace; his twin brother, Simon; and their older sister, Mallory. Tony and Holly visited them in Maine, and were shown "faerie artifacts"

as the kids told stories about what they had witnessed. The idea that these modern-day children were having adventures with faerie-tale characters fascinated Holly and Tony, and they turned the stories—with some changes and enhancements—into the wonderful five-book series, the Spiderwick Chronicles.

The books were a huge success, their small size and antique design attracting many readers of all ages, as did the unique stories, which combine modern-day kids dealing with realistic family problems and

a fantasy world that is based on centuries-old faerie folklore. Along with the success of the series came the idea for a movie based on the books. The challenge was to combine parts of all five books into one satisfying and visually appealing story!

The *Spiderwick Chronicles* is a movie about discovery—characters who discover an unseen, fantastical world and, at the same time, discover their family. It's a story about real kids who have to figure out how to battle trolls, ogres, and goblins. It's a journey that, in the end, brings a family together.

On the following pages readers will have a look behind the scenes and meet the dedicated people and production teams responsible for the creation of this wondrous movie.

In the early planning stages the idea was for the movie to tell just two of the five books in the Spiderwick Chronicles series because five felt like "too much for one movie," said Karey Kirkpatrick, one of the producers, who also cowrote the screenplay with John Sayles. However, because the five books told a complete story arc, it was decided that the movie needed to be adapted from all of them. "I think the challenge for the actors when you have a wealth of imaginative and great things to choose from is which ones you have to pull out," Karey added. "That's always the painful part."

KAREY KIRKPATRICK HAS WRITTEN A NUMBER OF SCREENPLAYS SINCE GRADUATING FROM THE UNIVERSITY OF SOUTHERN CALIFORNIA FILM SCHOOL. AMONG THEM ARE *CHARLOTTE'S WEB*; *OVER THE HEDGE*; *CHICKEN RUN*; *HONEY, WE SHRUNK OURSELVES*; *JAMES AND THE GIANT PEACH*; AND *THE HITCHHIKER'S GUIDE TO THE GALAXY*. HE ALSO DIRECTED *OVER THE HEDGE* (FOR WHICH HE WON AN ANNIE AWARD, THE HIGHEST HONOR FOR ANIMATED FEATURES) AND SERVED AS A CREATIVE CONSULTANT ON *MADAGASCAR*.

JOHN SAYLES IS WELL-KNOWN AS A NOVELIST, SCREENWRITER, AND FILMMAKER. HE IS THE DIRECTOR OF SIXTEEN MOVIES, INCLUDING *LONE STAR*, *EIGHT MEN OUT*, AND *THE SECRET OF ROAN INISH*. BORN IN UPSTATE NEW YORK, JOHN GRADUATED FROM WILLIAMS COLLEGE WITH A PSYCHOLOGY MAJOR. AT WILLIAMS HIS CLASSMATE WAS DAVID STRATHAIRN, WHO PLAYS ARTHUR SPIDERWICK! AMONG THE JOBS HE TOOK BEFORE BECOMING A FILMMAKER ARE A MEAT PACKER, CONSTRUCTION WORKER, FACTORY WORKER, AND NURSING-HOME ORDERLY.

OUTSIDE SPIDERWICK MANSION-NIGHT

Jared, Simon, Mallory, and their mother, Helen,
have just driven up to the fading Victorian mansion.

HELEN: There it is. Pretty much how I remember it.
       I was younger than you last time I
       was here, Simon.

MALLORY: It's . . . (searching for a nice word)
         big.

SIMON: Yeah. So I can get bigger pets here.
       Right, Mom?

HELEN: Sure. Get a cow. Get a whole flock.

SIMON: Herd.

HELEN: That, too.

The Story

Imagine what it would be like to suddenly move from a modern city into an old, weathered Victorian mansion in the middle of a forest! Mallory and her younger twin brothers, Simon and Jared, had to do just that, and they weren't too thrilled about it. They preferred New York City, but their mom and dad had split up, and now Helen Grace was forced to accept an invitation to live in the home of a distant relative, her eighty-six-year-old Aunt Lucinda. Aunt Lucinda herself had just moved into a nursing home.

When Helen and her children entered the mansion, they began an adventure that would change all of their lives. It started with Jared hearing noises and getting into trouble for banging on the walls with a broom. Then he was blamed for stealing the car keys and Mallory's fencing medal, which mysteriously turned up in a dumbwaiter. Knowing he was innocent, Jared was determined to find out who the *real* culprit was.

Armed with a flashlight and a key he had found,

Jared crawled into the dumbwaiter and pulled himself up toward the noises in the walls. At the top he found a room that was jam-packed with microscopes, magnifying glasses, and natural specimens. The secret study had belonged to Aunt Lucinda's father, Arthur Spiderwick, who disappeared when his daughter was just six years old. It was in this study that Jared found an old, leatherbound book—*Arthur Spiderwick's Field Guide to the Fantastical World Around You.* Although Jared had been warned not to read the book, he did anyway. It explained the strange things that had happened!

Without intending to, Arthur Spiderwick revealed many secrets of the faerie world, and in so doing had created a dangerous document within that world. The *Field Guide* had been hidden, sealed, and protected for several decades until Jared came along and opened it.

At first Mallory and Simon didn't believe what

their brother told them about all the creatures in the unseen world: brownies, boggarts, goblins, hobgoblin, phookas, sprites, and ogres. But when Simon was captured by goblins and Mallory engaged in a battle with the goblins, they finally realized that Jared had been right all along!

Mallory and Jared visited their great-aunt Lucinda, hoping that she could tell them what to do with the *Field Guide*. Aunt Lucinda knew why the ogre Mulgarath wanted the book for himself: so he could learn the secrets he needed to become powerful. And the only way Mulgarath could be stopped is if Jared brought the *Field Guide* to Arthur Spiderwick, and he destroyed it.

Realizing that he had put his family in

danger, Jared had to rely on his wits to make things right. Following the defense methods described in the *Field Guide*, Jared and his family prepared to protect the mansion against the inevitable attack from the goblins and Mulgarath. They were still getting ready when the ten-foot Mulgarath and the goblins broke through the Protective Circle and burst into the house.

The shape-shifting Mulgarath chased Jared to grab the *Field Guide* from him. And as Jared tossed it, Mulgarath transformed into a crow. But before he could snatch the book, Hogsqueal the hobgoblin gobbled up the bird in two bites!

In the end it was Jared's persistence and love for his family that saved them from disaster, uniting them so they could all begin their new life together in the Spiderwick Mansion.

The Location
MONTREAL

The *Spiderwick Chronicles* is set in New England, but was filmed in the eastern Canadian city of Montreal. After getting permission to knock down a small shack in a park called Cap St. Jacques, the complete exterior of the elaborate mansion was built in the middle of the forest. Its fourth story was the tower the kids climb to when the house is surrounded by goblins.

Shooting on location presented many challenges, especially with Montreal's unpredictable weather. As it turned out, most of the outside scenes were filmed during the rainiest October on record. Imagine what it was like with a crew of more than a hundred people slogging through the mud every day, doing dolly shots and moving lighting equipment.

Some interiors were built outside as well, but most were built on a soundstage, making the weather

elements easier to control. These included the set where Mulgarath crashed through the house, as well as the goblin camp, which would have been difficult to shoot outside at night. Some of the sets shown toward the end of the movie were also created digitally.

THE ROCKS IN THE GOBLINS' CAMP LOOK REAL BUT THEY'RE NOT! ALL THE SHAPES AND FORMS OF THE ROCKS ARE PREDESIGNED BY THE PRODUCTION DESIGN TEAM AND SET DESIGNER. THE ROCKS ARE ACTUALLY A LAYER OF CEMENT ON TOP OF A WIRE MESH AND WOODEN FRAME. THE CEMENT MAKES IT ROCK-HARD, BUT THE ROCKS ARE HOLLOW! THE LEAVES ON THE TREES AND SHRUBS ARE ALSO NOT REAL. THE GOBLIN CAMP IS COVERED WITH THOUSANDS OF PLASTIC LEAVES, AND THEY'RE ATTACHED TO REAL BRANCHES.

The Mansion

"I've never seen a more beautiful place in my life. The leaves were all golden and red. It was just the perfect place for the Spiderwick Mansion."
—Sarah Bolger

Angela DiTerlizzi

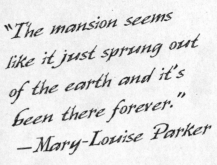

The Director
MARK WATERS

"I saw this as an opportunity to do a movie that dealt with adventure, fantasy, and incredible, interesting creatures but wasn't set in some far-off land with British wizards or gothic orphans. Instead there were these very identifiable American kids who just seemed like they got plunked down in an extremely extraordinary situation."

—Mark Waters

Mark Waters, the director of *The Spiderwick Chronicles*, also directed *Mean Girls* and *Freaky Friday*. He worked as an actor and theater director in San Francisco after graduating from the University of Pennsylvania in 1986. After several years on stage, he decided to earn his MFA in directing from the American Film Institute. In 1997 he made his directorial debut with *The House of Yes*, starring Freddie Prinze Jr. and Parker Posey. Based on a stage play, Waters adapted the script into a screenplay. The film received various award nominations from festivals and won Special Recognition at Sundance for Posey's performance.

Known for being fantastic with young actors, Mark earned high praise from

Freddie Highmore and Sarah Bolger.

"Mark is a fun guy to have on set," Freddie said. "He's always cheerful and energetic." Freddie also felt that Mark helped a lot in figuring out the best approach to playing twins.

"Mark Waters is an amazing director," said Sarah. "He's very patient. He's great at giving direction, and at the same time he's very open to new ideas."

She and Freddie enjoyed having Mark play the roles of creatures like Mulgarath, since the voice actors weren't around during filming.

"He's so great to be around that he just makes you want to come to work," Mary-Louise Parker said.

"Mark approaches the film in a very funny way," said Pablo Helman, who was in charge of the visual effects. "He's an actor's director, and he also is very collaborative when it comes to visual effects."

"We basically all collaborate," said Michael Lantieri, the supervisor of special effects,

"Throughout the entire process, Mark continually upheld the themes—both written and visual—that we worked so hard to put into the books. As the creator, you can't ask for much more."

—Tony DiTerlizzi

"and then as a director Mark has kind of the final word. Everything goes by Mark, and everything is approved by him."

For *The Spiderwick Chronicles* everyone agreed that Mark assembled an amazing cast and crew.

"Do not dare to read this book
For if you take one fateful look,
You barter at your life's expense
And face a deadly consequence."

WARNING!
DO NOT READ

The Cast

Jared/Simon Grace	FREDDIE HIGHMORE
Helen Grace	MARY-LOUISE PARKER
Mulgarath	NICK NOLTE
Lucinda Spiderwick	JOAN PLOWRIGHT
Arthur Spiderwick	DAVID STRATHAIRN
Hogsqueal	SETH ROGEN (voice)
Thimbletack	MARTIN SHORT (voice)
Mallory Grace	SARAH BOLGER
Richard Grace	ANDREW MCCARTHY
Young Lucinda Spiderwick	JORDY BENATTAR

Jared and Simon Grace
FREDDIE HIGHMORE

Freddie Highmore was cast as twins Simon and Jared Grace. It was quite a challenge to play twins who are nothing alike! Simon is quiet, scientific, and an animal lover. Jared is troubled, angry, and rebellious—quite different from Freddie's roles in *Charlie and the Chocolate Factory* and *Finding Neverland*. Each twin reacted to his parents' breakup in different ways: Jared acted out and blamed his mom for their separation while Simon escaped into his books and thoughts.

HOW DID FREDDIE MAKE THE TWINS DIFFERENT?

"It was good fun to do both parts. Jared and Simon are on opposite sides of the same coin. The one thing we had to do was to try and make the brothers as different as possible so there's never confusion about who it could be. Their dad has left, and Jared reacts with anger, and he totally thinks it's his mom's fault. Simon is just as upset, but he doesn't show it in the same way. Jared's look is a red

FREDDIE WAS BORN IN 1992 IN LONDON. HIS GIVEN NAME IS ALFRED THOMAS HIGHMORE. HE LIVES IN THE LONDON SUBURB OF HIGHGATE WITH HIS MOM, DAD, AND BROTHER, BERTIE.

hooded sweatshirt and jeans. Simon is better dressed, with a shirt with a collar, and corduroys."

HOW DID FREDDIE PLAY JARED AND SIMON IN THE SAME SCENE?

"If Jared and Simon are in the same shot, that can work quite well because I know what the other person is going to be doing. They had other actors play the part of one of the brothers. If I'm Simon, they play Jared, and if I play Jared, they play Simon. When the brothers are in the same shot, then what they'll do is shoot the scene with the person who has a bigger role in it; they're shot first with all the other characters around them, and they do a separate thing where the camera does exactly the same

thing, and then they do the other character walking by. And later the shot is edited with the stand-in character taken out and Jared or Simon Grace put in his place."

WHICH SEQUENCE WAS MOST FUN TO FILM?

"It was fun to do this thing where I was Simon, and I was outside, walking along, calling for Mr. Tibbs, the cat, so he

can have his breakfast. And then I fall to the ground and get turned over by goblins. They attached these things to my legs, which pulled my legs, flipped me around, onto my back and onto my front, and then dragged me away!"

AUDITIONING

Freddie goes to a normal private school in London, and took a break from school to come to the United States. to promote one of his other movies. While he was here, he was called to do a screen test in L.A. for *Spiderwick*. "It was quite appealing because you get to play the two characters, Jared and Simon," Freddie said. After two weeks he found out he got the part!

SCHOOLING ON THE SET

"I had to do three hours of school a day. A tutor came from London to do the school

work, so I was doing pretty much the same stuff that people do at school. After the three hours of school we went on to the set, got into makeup and then hair, and then got into costume, and then normally there was a bit of time and we got some more schooling in, and then went to the set and had lunch, and did a bit more school until the end of the day."

Mallory Grace
SARAH BOLGER

Sarah Bolger, from Dublin, Ireland, plays Mallory Grace, the older sister. Mallory carries a sword in every scene, and keeps the secret of her parents' breakup from her twin brothers. "She's a lovely young actress," said Andrew McCarthy, who was a big fan of Sarah and her sister, Emma, in the movie *In America*.

"She has an incredible technique for someone her age," says Mary-Louise Parker, who played Helen Grace, her mother in the movie. Sarah's real-life mother, Monica, and her sister came with her to Montreal.

FENCING

Sarah took about two months of fencing lessons before she came on the set, training with Dominique Tesser who trains the Canadian fencing team. "I have to say, it's great fun," Sarah said. "Mallory has amazing scenes where she's fencing and slashing goblins and things like that."

The swords used are not actual fencing foils or sabers.

BORN IN 1991, SARAH HAS ACTED WITH HER YOUNGER SISTER, EMMA, IN *IN AMERICA*, WHERE THEY PLAYED SISTERS.

"They're made of very light metal. There are some fake ones to use especially when we're running . . . so it wouldn't be a huge problem if anyone fell. But they look very real, and they're light because at the end of the day your arm would get tired."

AMERICAN ACCENT!

"I came here three weeks before shooting, and Freddie and I started with the dialect coach to try and make sure there was no hint of our Irish or English accents. During the film it's been great fun to have a different accent and be that different person."

Helen Grace
MARY-LOUISE PARKER

Sheryl Nields

Mary-Louise Parker is the actress who portrays Helen Grace, a woman who recently separated from her husband. Determined to make their new life work, Helen and her children moved to Spiderwick Mansion, the home of a distant relative.

An award-winning actress, Mary-Louise is currently seen as a frazzled mom on the TV series *Weeds*. She said she felt drawn to *Spiderwick* because it was an emotional and character-driven film.

Mary-Louise majored in drama at the North Carolina School of the Arts. Since her start in a small role on the soap opera *Ryan's Hope*, the actress has appeared on Broadway, and in numerous movies and TV series such as *Fried Green Tomatoes*, *Boys on the Side*, *Proof*, *The West Wing*, *Angels in America*, *Grand Canyon*, and *Weeds*.

"Mary-Louise Parker is a phenomenal actress, and I've just been overjoyed to have a chance to work with her."
—Mark Waters

Aunt Lucinda
JOAN PLOWRIGHT

Joan Plowright is Aunt Lucinda, the daughter of Arthur Spiderwick, who invited the Grace family to live in her mansion. Her father had told her bedtime stories about the faerie world, and she eventually went to live in a sanitarium because her visions of faeries convinced people that she was crazy. Best known as a theater actress, Joan played her character brilliantly, with the perfect blend of nuttiness and authority. The award-winning actress has had roles in a number of children's films, including *Curious George* and Disney's *101 Dalmatians*.

Born in England, Joan was married to the legendary actor Sir Laurence Olivier. Their three children, Richard, Tamsin, and Julie Kate, also went into the family business.

Young Lucinda
JORDY BENATTAR

Jordy was born in 1993 in Toronto, Canada, and has appeared in a number of TV movies.

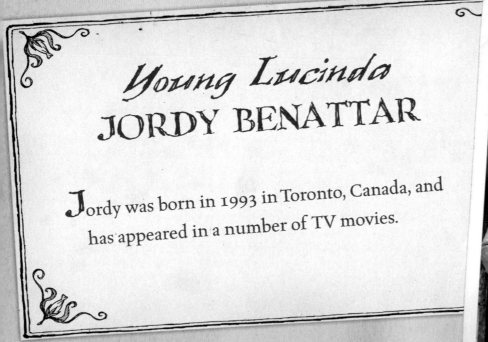

© 2006 Getty Images

Arthur Spiderwick
DAVID STRATHAIRN

David Strathairn portrays Helen Grace's great-great uncle, Arthur Spiderwick, the naturalist who devoted his life to creating the *Field Guide* so others would believe in a parallel faerie world. David received an Oscar® nomination for *Good Night, and Good Luck*. What he liked most about working on this movie was the chance to "work with goblins"!

A native of California, David attended Williams College, and later the Ringling Brothers Clown College in Florida. He worked as a clown for six months before moving to New York, and then hitchhiking across America to work in local theaters during the summers. During one of these summers he reunited with his college friend, John Sayles, who directed him in the highly regarded *Return of the Secaucus 7*. David lives with his wife and two children in upstate New York.

Richard Grace
ANDREW MCCARTHY

Andrew McCarthy is Richard Grace, the dad of Jared, Simon, and Mallory. Though the role was small, Andrew McCarthy found his character to have "a lot of nooks and crannies" in him. Many agreed that he actually looked like he could be Freddie Highmore's real dad.

Andrew began acting when he was a teenager, performing in plays and musicals at the Pingry School, a prep school in New Jersey. Majoring in theater at New York University, he has also studied at the Circle in the Square Theater School in New York.

Andrew has appeared in many movies, including *St. Elmo's Fire*, *Less Than Zero*, *Pretty in Pink*, *Weekend at Bernie's*, *Mannequin*, and *The Joy Luck Club*.

THE ACTORS CAST IN THE MOVIE LOOK A LOT LIKE THE WAY HOLLY BLACK AND TONY DITERLIZZI ORIGINALLY PICTURED THEM!

The Production Team

It took a talented team of experts to bring *Spiderwick* to life. Many of them worked together in the past and have great respect for each other's work. The different departments communicated with each other often as they strove to make a very special movie that met the director's vision.

MARK CANTON is one of the producers of *The Spiderwick Chronicles*. He comes up with ideas, works with actors, and supervises shooting. Mark got his start in the movie business when he worked in the mail room at Warner Brothers. He later became an executive vice president of worldwide motion picture production for the company! Mark's work can be seen in *Gremlins*, *Goonies*, *Jack Frost*, and *300*, which was also filmed in Montreal and filled with special effects.

"I've never seen a crew and a group of people like this who are this professional and this experienced."
—*Mark Canton, Producer*

LARRY FRANCO, another producer, is a California native and graduated from the UCLA film school and the Director's Guild of America Training Program. He started working as an assistant director with filmmaker John Carpenter, and went on to produce many of Carpenter's other films as well. Larry also served as producer for films such as *Jurassic Park III*, *Mars Attacks!*, *Jumanji*, *Batman Returns*, and *The Rocketeer*.

ELLEN GOLDSMITH-VEIN was working as an investment banker for a long time before she decided to invest in her creative side and founded the Gotham Group, an agency that today represents more than 250 top filmmakers, producers, illustrators, and writers. Besides *The Spiderwick Chronicles*, Ellen will also produce a number of upcoming movies, including *Stargirl; A Great and Terrible Beauty;* and *Here, There Be Dragons.*

JIM BISSELL is the production designer. A graduate of the University of North Carolina, he was also involved in the making of *300*. He has won the Satellite Award for Outstanding Art Direction & Production Design for *Good Night, and Good Luck*. He has also worked on *Cats & Dogs, Jumanji, Dennis the Menace,* and *Arachnophobia*. In many of his movies Jim's greatest challenges are making everything seem real, and the computer-animated characters seem like a natural part of the world.

Angela DiTerlizzi

JAMES HORNER is the composer who wrote original music for the movie. Winner of the Oscar® and Golden Globe awards for the original score and song for *Titanic*, James's career in the movie music world began with low-budget horror assignments. Then he began scoring student films for the American Film Institute, which led to scoring assignments on a number of small-scale films and then major motion pictures. The movies he has scored include *Cocoon, Willow, Field of Dreams, A Beautiful Mind, Star Trek II* and *III, Braveheart,* and *Apollo 13*.

> "Jim was able to take our theme of 'man versus nature,' and integrate it into every visual facet, from the oak leaf motif in the glass transom of the house, to the trees growing up and out of the junked cars in the goblins' camp."
> —Tony DiTerlizzi

© 2004 Getty Images

The Creatures

As the character designer and animation supervisor, Phil Tippett is in charge of making the creatures in *The Spiderwick Chronicles* come to life! Pablo Helman of Industrial Light and Magic is in charge of the visual effects. They worked closely together to create digital goblins, ogres, faeries, sprites, and the other magical creatures.

Their teams also created maquettes and models of the creatures that the actors worked with. These versions varied from cardboard versions on poles which were carried around by people, to more fully molded characters that were placed on a tree and set down.

Karey Kirkpatrick, one of the producers of the movie, said, "It's actually hard when you're doing a movie like this and you've got Pablo and his team chasing you with a cardboard goblin on a stick to not look back and laugh. You realize that you're actually supposed to be terrified. But that's acting!"

The founder of Tippett Studios, Phil has been involved with some of the most successful movies of all time, including *Star Wars Episode V–The Empire Strikes Back, Star Wars:*

Episode VI: Return of the Jedi, My Favorite Martian, Willow, Jurassic Park, and Charlotte's Web. He won an Oscar® for Best Visual Effects for Jurassic Park, as well as a Special Achievement Award for Return of the Jedi.

Among the many movies that Pablo Helman has worked on are Munich, War of the Worlds, Star Wars Episode I: The Phantom Menace, Star Wars Episode II: Attack of the Clones, Space Cowboys, Saving Private Ryan, Contact, The Lost World: Jurassic Park, and Men in Black. He received Oscar® nominations for his work on Attack of the Clones and War of the Worlds.

HOW TIPPETT STUDIOS BEGAN

While Phil Tippett worked at Industrial Light and Magic (ILM), he codeveloped the revolutionary stop-motion technique called go-motion, which was used in Dragonslayer and Star Wars Episode VI: Return of the Jedi. In 1983 he left ILM and founded Tippett Studios in Berkley, California, which is now one of the leading visual effects houses specializing in 3-D CGI character animation. It was there that Phil created the spectacular dinosaur effects for Steven Spielberg's Jurassic Park.

When Phil heard the Jurassic Park dinosaurs would be computer-generated, he said, "I've just become extinct." But because of his background and understanding of animal movement and behavior, Spielberg kept Phil on to supervise the animation of the dinosaurs in Jurassic Park.

Actors supplied the voices for each creature, and these recording sessions were filmed. Phil Tippett and Pablo Helman watched footage of these recordings so that they could study

the actors' facial expressions. Then their teams took images from the recordings and mimicked the expressions of the actors onto the digital creatures. That way the creatures were each given its own distinct personality. The main creatures ranged in size from nine-inch Thimbletack to ten-foot Mulgarath.

All characters were completely computer-generated. Some, such as Mulgarath, occasionally involved a human actor (Nick Nolte) with CGI enhancement for transformations. The actor wore a mask and his lines were read off screen. Then ILM replaced the actor's hands and face with the digital images of the character he was playing.

The Fantastical Creatures of
THE SPIDERWICK CHRONICLES

Thimbletack

Mulgarath

Hogsqueal

Griffin

Redcap

Goblins

Sprites

Thimbletack
MARTIN SHORT

Martin Short is the voice of Thimbletack, the loyal house brownie. An Emmy award-winning comedian, actor, writer, and producer, Martin was originally planning to be a social worker, but he became interested in acting when he was cast in a Toronto production of *Godspell*. He has acted in such movies as *The Santa Clause 3: The Escape Clause* and *Mars Attacks!*, and provided the voices for characters in *101 Dalmatians II: Patch's London Adventure*, *Treasure Planet*, and *Jimmy Neutron: Boy Genius*. Martin lives in California but also has a home in Canada, where he has a star on Canada's Walk of Fame.

Hogsqueal
SETH ROGEN

Seth Rogen is the voice of Hogsqueal. A native of Canada, Seth did standup comedy for four years when he was a teenager, finishing second in the Vancouver Amateur Comedy Contest when he was sixteen.

Seth provided the voice of the Ship Captain in *Shrek the Third*, and also has a role in

Horton Hears a Who. The popular actor has acted in many TV series, including *Freaks and Geeks*, *Undeclared*, and *Dawson's Creek*. He's also appeared in movies such as *Donnie Darko*; *You, Me, and Dupree*; and *Anchorman: The Legend of Ron Burgundy*.

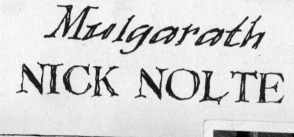

"Phil's team understood that these creatures were not cartoon characters running about on the screen—they had to be convincing in every aspect. We wanted the audience to believe there could be a brownie just like Thimbletack, that goblins could be rummaging in the woods, and there may just be faeries fluttering about when no one is looking."

—Tony DiTerlizzi

Mulgarath
NICK NOLTE

Nick Nolte is Mulgarath, the evil, ten-foot, shapeshifting ogre. A veteran of the movie business, Nick has starred in more than forty films, playing a variety of characters, and is best known for his roles in *Affliction*, *The Prince of Tides*, *The Thin Red Line*, and *48 Hours*. After getting his start as a model in Minneapolis, Minnesota, Nick took to the stage at the Pasadena Playhouse and in regional theater productions. His breakout role was in the TV miniseries, *Rich Man, Poor Man*. The award-winning actor also appeared in *Hotel Rwanda*, *Hulk*, and played the voice of Vincent in *Over the Hedge*.

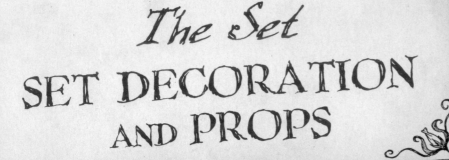

The Set
SET DECORATION
AND PROPS

"You always imagine what it would be like to be able to walk into a book, and this is probably about as close as anybody could ever get."

—Holly Black

In the movie Jared stumbles into a room that's jam-packed with microscopes, magnifying glasses, and natural specimens. The secret study belonged to Arthur Spiderwick, who was a naturalist in the early 1900s. Spiderwick believed he had made a magnificent discovery: the ability to see into the fascinating faerie world. But no one took him seriously. Hoping to convince others of its existence, he observed the magical creatures, illustrated them, and recorded their powers, strengths, and weaknesses in a field guide. The set

decorators, Jan Pascal and Paul Hotte, spent three months going to flea markets and estate sales, and perusing eBay, putting together a fantastic collection of items to capture the essence of Arthur Spiderwick's study.

Sometimes the characters dictated what the spaces would be like. Some ceilings in the mansion had to be high enough for Mulgarath to wander through the house, destroying doorways and furniture along the way. Thimbletack, on the other hand, was less than nine inches tall, so his world was much smaller, yet there still had to be a lot of detail in his miniature environment.

Many versions of the dumbwaiter were created. One was part of the kitchen set. Another, which was on a platform, showed Jared going up to the secret study. As he pulled the rope, the background moved up and down. This was done so the cameraman wouldn't have to constantly crane up and down twenty feet. There was also a tiny

"I think the secret study is just extraordinary. Tony [DiTerlizzi] said that he wanted to move in and make that his study. So I took that as the best compliment because I certainly admire his work a lot, and if he's comfortable there, then I don't think we could hope for more."

—Jim Bissell

dumbwaiter for the close-ups of Thimbletack and his nest.

Property master Claire Alary was in charge of all of the handheld props, which are the props that tell the story, as opposed to decorative props. The handheld props included the Seeing Stone and the *Field Guide*, the movie's most important prop. Many people worked on the *Guide*, including a calligrapher, so the handwriting would look just right. A few versions of the book were made, including a wet one and one with everything in it, which is the one Jared read. It contained a detailed map of the fantastical world, and was also filled with characters from existing faerie lore.

The Special Effects

"I think the biggest challenge for actors working in an effects-driven movie is playing to a character that's not there."

—Michael Lantieri, Special Effects Supervisor

As the special effects supervisor, Michael Lantieri worked closely with Phil Tippett and Pablo Helman. While their work was all computer-generated, Michael made physical things happen—like explosions and door jambs breaking. Together they planned such details as whether Thimbletack was a righty or lefty, and the size of Mulgarath's footsteps. Michael's goal was to make everything seem as if it's happening inside a real environment. A native of California, Michael has worked on movies such as *Superman Returns*, *Pirates of the Caribbean: Dead Man's Chest*, *Lemony Snicket's A Series of Unfortunate Events*, *The Polar Express*, *Seabiscuit*, *Jurassic Park*, *A.I. Artificial Intelligence*, *Mars Attacks!*, and *Matilda*. The awards he has received for his work include an Oscar® for Best Visual Effects for *The Lost World: Jurassic Park*; and two Saturn Awards for Best Special Effects for

Jurassic Park and A.I. Artificial Intelligence.

SEEING THE CREATURES

In the movie the Seeing Stone allowed the Grace family to see elves, goblins, faeries, and sprites. But the actual actors saw nothing! In scenes where they interacted with a creature, a cardboard cutout on a stick or a created model was used in place of the computer-generated image so the actors knew where to focus. This is called an "eye line."

"They were basically looking straight through something that's going to be put in later," Michael noted.

THE DUMBWAITER

Freddie Highmore found filming in the dumbwaiter to be quite an experience. "It was quite weird because I would sit in there and they just moved the walls around me and the rope, so it looks like I'm going up, but actually I'm just staying level so the camera can be with me the whole time. It's a bit like going in a car. You know you're still,

"It's very strange, those little cardboard pieces coming toward you. At the same time I was very careful because there were people behind the creatures. I didn't want to hit them with the sword. The cardboard creatures on sticks represent what the goblin is going to be doing. [The crew] created where they wanted to place the goblins when they're computerized."

—Sarah Bolger

and then you realize you're whizzing along. It wasn't too claustrophobic because most of the time they have at least a few sides open so they can fit the cameras in it. It's not like being in a little box."

SPITTING

Sarah and Freddie had fun shooting the scenes where Hogsqueal spat in their faces. "[The crew] hit us in the head, ear, and body, and it didn't really go to the eye," explained Freddie. "In the end we just put some gloop in our hands."

The actual flying spit was computer-generated.

FIGHTING WITH GOBLINS

Early on in the movie production process, Michael Lantieri sat down with Caleb Deschanel, the director of photography, to talk about creating atmosphere, such as smoke, fog, wind, and rain. A five-time Oscar® nominee, Caleb was responsible for *Spiderwick*'s dark look. Some of his other credits include *Fly Away Home*, *The Black Stallion*, *The Right Stuff*, *The Natural*, and *The Passion of the Christ*.

CALEB DESCHANEL IS MARRIED TO THE ACTRESS MARY JO DESCHANEL AND IS THE FATHER OF ACTRESSES EMILY DESCHANEL AND ZOOEY DESCHANEL, WHO VOICED THE CHARACTER OF LANI IN *SURF'S UP*, AND IS WELL-KNOWN FOR HER ROLE IN *ELF*. SHE HAS ALSO APPEARED WITH MARY-LOUISE PARKER IN *WEEDS*.

And Action!

David McKeown is the stunt coordinator, and he was kept very busy on *The Spiderwick Chronicles*, as it is filled with live-action stunts! "When you think things are going to slow down, they pick up once again," David said. He made sure that the kids stayed safe "and that they didn't hurt any of the goblins."

For tricky stunts, like Mallory fighting against goblins who weren't there, Phil Tippett and Pablo Helman helped to marry the visual and the actual physical effects together. When the kids fell down in the woods, it was a combination of stunts and visual effects.

DAVID HAS WORKED AS A STUNTMAN AND AS A STUNT COORDINATOR ON A NUMBER OF MOVIES, INCLUDING JUMANJI, THE NOTEBOOK, DAWN OF THE DEAD, THE AVIATOR, ROLLERBALL, AND SHANGHAI NOON.

HOW A STUNT IS DONE:

- The director shares his vision with the stunt coordinator, with specific directions about where he wants the character to start and to end up.
- The stunt coordinator works out a plan.
- Rigging for the stunt is created with climbing ropes, wire, or whatever is needed for sliding down a roof, a free fall, or any other type of stunt.
- The actors or stunt doubles are given specific instructions.
- The scene is shot—often a number of times!

"All of a sudden goblins keep popping up through the floor-boards, and we had to try and stamp down on them. We had so much fun doing it."

—Sarah Bolger

In one scene the piano was about to pin the Grace family against the wall. "It was pretty unbelievable," said Mary-Louise Parker. "Even though you know the piano's going to stop before it gets to you, it just doesn't seem like it's going to."

The kitchen scene was all done with special effects while the kids were hiding from the explosion. In the hallway scene visual and physical effects were used as the young actors and their stunt doubles fought the goblins when they entered the house. Mallory was thrown across the room and through the banister. Simon slammed into his mother.

FILMING ON THE ROOF!

Toward the end of the movie, when Mulgarath chased Jared up to the roof of the mansion in an attempt to get the *Field Guide*, Jared struggled,

AS THE LEAD STUNT DOUBLE, EIGHTEEN-YEAR-OLD PASCAL ARCHAMBAULT SERVED AS FREDDIE'S STUNT DOUBLE IN THE MOVIE. HERE HE'S FILMING THE EXCITING ROOF SCENE. BUT FREDDIE IS VERY ATHLETIC AND DID MANY OF HIS OWN STUNTS AS WELL.

fought, and then fell off the roof. Rigging specialist André Laperrière rigged this scene to be shot in different stages. In the rooftop scenes where Jared interacts with Mulgarath, a stunt double for Freddie was used. So it was his stunt double who fell off the house, but Mulgarath grabbed the line and stopped him from plummeting to the ground!

In closeup shots Freddie was filmed on the set or against a green screen, with the digital creature and background added to the film later. This exciting climactic scene had Jared tossing the *Guide* into the air, and Mulgarath letting go of the wire. He transformed into a crow to fly after the *Guide*. Jared ended up hanging about three feet off the ground as he watched Hogsqueal devour the bird.

Until about six weeks before filming was about to begin, the setting of the ending was not finalized. Karey Kirkpatrick recalled, "We actually got some smart people to discuss what would be the

most satisfying place to set this.
And unanimously everybody said,
'Let's do a siege on the house.' This book was found in the house, the whole movie has been goblins surrounding this protective circle, trying to get in; let's compromise the circle and get in the house."

So the teams had to figure out a way to "dramatically have these guys busting in this house. So goblins come up through the floorboards, the ceiling . . . and Mulgarath makes his dramatic entrance."

And the ogre exited just as dramatically, bringing a very satisfying end to the story!

KYLE SWITZER, SEEN IN THE PHOTO BELOW, OFTEN PROVIDED OFF-CAMERA DIALOGUE FOR THE CG CHARACTERS.

"You are the book now. And that knowledge is very powerful. Use it wisely."

—Arthur Spiderwick to Jared Grace